IT'S TIME TO EAT GRAPES

It's Time to Eat GRAPES

Walter the Educator

Silent King Books
A WhichHead Entertainment Imprint

Copyright © 2024 by Walter the Educator

All rights reserved. No part of this book may be reproduced in any manner whatsoever without written per- mission except in the case of brief quotations embodied in critical articles and reviews.

First Printing, 2024

Disclaimer

This book is a literary work; the story is not about specific persons, locations, situations, and/or circumstances unless mentioned in a historical context. Any resemblance to real persons, locations, situations, and/or circumstances is coincidental. This book is for entertainment and informational purposes only. The author and publisher offer this information without warranties expressed or implied. No matter the grounds, neither the author nor the publisher will be accountable for any losses, injuries, or other damages caused by the reader's use of this book. The use of this book acknowledges an understanding and acceptance of this disclaimer.

It's Time to Eat GRAPES is a collectible early learning book by Walter the Educator suitable for all ages belonging to Walter the Educator's Time to Eat Book Series. Collect more books at WaltertheEducator.com

USE THE EXTRA SPACE TO TAKE NOTES AND DOCUMENT YOUR MEMORIES

GRAPES

It's time to eat, come take a look,

It's Time to Eat

Grapes

Grapes are waiting in the nook!

Green or purple, red or gold,

A juicy snack that never gets old.

Tiny and round, they fit your hand,

Grapes are the best, isn't that grand?

Pop them in, they're sweet and fun,

A treat for all, for everyone!

Crunchy skins and soft inside,

Each little grape is a yummy ride.

Cold and fresh, they taste so neat,

Oh, how grapes make life so sweet!

Pluck them gently from the vine,

They grow in rows, all in a line.

Bunches of grapes, so many to share,

A gift from nature, beyond compare!

It's Time to Eat

Grapes

Eat them plain or in a dish,

Grapes are yummy, just as you wish!

Make some juice or jelly too,

Grapes can do so much for you.

Packed with goodness, energy,

Grapes help keep you strong, you'll see!

With every bite, you'll smile so wide,

A grape-filled day feels good inside.

Grapes are tiny, but don't be fooled,

They're full of vitamins, so cool!

Healthy, tasty, fresh, and small,

Grapes are the snack that has it all.

Keep them cold or in a bowl,

Grab a bunch, they make you whole.

Morning, evening, or midday,

It's Time to Eat

Grapes

Grapes are perfect any way!

So let's enjoy this special treat,

A grape or two is fun to eat.

Pop them in and feel the cheer,

Grapes bring smiles all through the year!

One for you and one for me,

Let's share them happily under a tree.

It's grape time now, let's not wait,

It's Time to Eat

Grapes

A snack so good, it's truly great!

ABOUT THE CREATOR

Walter the Educator is one of the pseudonyms for Walter Anderson. Formally educated in Chemistry, Business, and Education, he is an educator, an author, a diverse entrepreneur, and he is the son of a disabled war veteran. "Walter the Educator" shares his time between educating and creating. He holds interests and owns several creative projects that entertain, enlighten, enhance, and educate, hoping to inspire and motivate you. Follow, find new works, and stay up to date with Walter the Educator™

at WaltertheEducator.com

www.ingramcontent.com/pod-product-compliance
Lightning Source LLC
LaVergne TN
LVHW010623070526
838199LV00063BA/5250